WALKS FOR ALL AGES
WILTSHIRE

WALKS *FOR* ALL **AGES**

WILTSHIRE

RACHAEL ROWE

BRADWELL
BOOKS

Published by Bradwell Books
9 Orgreave Close Sheffield S13 9NP
Email: books@bradwellbooks.co.uk

1st Edition

ISBN: 9781909914704

Print: Gomer Press, Llandysul, Ceredigion SA44 4JL

Design by: Andrew Caffrey. Typesetting by: Erik Siewko Creative

Photograph Credits: © D. Day

Maps: Contain Ordnance Survey data
© Crown copyright and database right 2014

Ordnance Survey licence number 100039353

The information in this book has been produced in good faith and is intended as a general guide. Bradwell Books and its authors have made all reasonable efforts to ensure that the details are correct at the time of publication. Bradwell Books and the author cannot accept any responsibility for any changes that have taken place subsequent to the book being published. It is the responsibility of individuals undertaking any of the walks listed in this publication to exercise due care and consideration for the health and wellbeing of each other in the party. Particular care should be taken if you are inexperienced. The walks in this book are not especially strenuous but individuals taking part should ensure they are fit and able to complete the walk before setting off.

WALKS FOR ALL AGES

Walk 1	Fovant	6 miles	p. 8
Walk 2	Old Sarum	2 miles	p. 14
Walk 3	Avebury	6 miles	p. 18
Walk 4	Berwick St James	5 miles	p. 22
Walk 5	Steeple Ashton and Keevil	4 miles	p. 26
Walk 6	Mere	5 miles	p. 30
Walk 7	Langley Burrell	2½ miles	p. 34
Walk 8	Corsham	4 miles	p. 38
Walk 9	Biddestone	4 miles	p. 42
Walk 10	Downton	4 miles	p. 46
Walk 11	Great Bedwyn	5 miles	p. 50
Walk 12	Cricklade	3 miles	p. 54
Walk 13	Barbury Castle	4 miles	p. 58
Walk 14	Tisbury	4 miles	p. 64
Walk 15	Heytesbury	5 miles	p. 68
Walk 16	Marlborough	2 miles	p. 72
Walk 17	Durrington	4 miles	p. 76
Walk 18	Bradford-on-Avon	4 miles	p. 80
Walk 19	Malmesbury	4 miles	p. 86
Walk 20	Roundway Hill	4 miles	p. 92

INTRODUCTION

Wiltshire is a county steeped in ancient legend and intriguing history and has some of the most dramatic scenery in the South West. There are white horses, mysterious stone circles and weathered sarsen stones as well as delightful villages to discover.

It is all too easy to drive straight through Wiltshire with a cursory nod to Stonehenge on the A303. But take a walk here and you'll feel the essence of the county and discover those unique features and welcoming neighbourhoods. This is a county where eight white horses stand proud on the hills and where ancient hill-farming tracts can still be seen on the landscape. It has villages that take pride in their historic blind houses or lock-ups and where medieval tithe barns have seen the harvest gathered in from the fields. Walk across a water meadow in Downton and you can discover the legacy and heritage of the drowners who expertly managed the floodplains.

Walks in Wiltshire have inspired writers to create prose and define places like Scratchbury Camp which are forever immortalised in poetry. This is where war poets like Edward Thomas and Siegfried Sassoon spent their days on the eve of World War I and where Richard Jefferies captured the spirit of the Marlborough Downs. In the quiet villages of Fovant and Sutton Veny there are reminders of World War I and the troops that were stationed in the Wylie Valley, now remembered in the cemeteries and by the regimental badges on the hills.

Devizes is a beautiful town in Wiltshire famed for its locks and overlooked by Roundaway Hill where a decisive battle took place in the English Civil War. At Salisbury the cathedral spire dominates the landscape and is overlooked by Old Sarum, the ancient settlement now in ruins. Wiltshire's heritage combines the quaintness of Great Bedwyn's stonemasonry with the engineering genius of the Kennet and Avon Canal and the railway works at Swindon. It is epitomised in the legacy of Maud Heath's Causeway where a simple good deed helped people for generations to come.

To walk in Wiltshire is to discover a county that radiates joy and has a welcome in its villages and towns for visitors. From the hill forts of Barbury Castle to watching great bustards on Salisbury Plain, a walk in this county is a fine way to experience its heritage and landscapes.

FOVANT

FOVANT IS A PRETTY VILLAGE NEAR SALISBURY, NESTLED IN THE NADDER VALLEY. THE NAME IS DERIVED FROM THE OLD ENGLISH FOBBEFUNTA, WHICH MEANS 'SPRING OF A MAN CALLED FOBBE'.

This walk will take you along country lanes and across Fovant Down in an area known for dramatic hillsides and distinctive regimental badges from World War I as well as a historic hill fort. There are stunning views and poignant memories here on this picturesque Wiltshire walk.

During World War I land and property was commandeered as barracks, hospitals and training grounds in Wiltshire. The village of Fovant, along with neighbouring communities, became a military camp and there was also a hospital for troops on Fovant Down. Many men passed through Fovant on their way to the trenches, as a railway line transported them to and from the south coast of England. Sadly, many never returned to their homelands. Several men also died in the influenza epidemic of 1919. Today Fovant Churchyard is the last resting place of men from all over the Commonwealth who fought in World War I.

The first badge to appear on Fovant Downs was constructed during 1916 when troops from the London Rifle Brigade garrisoned in the area carved their regimental insignia into the hillside. This was so successful that others soon followed. By the end of the war there were badges spread out across Fovant Down from the Australian Commonwealth Military Forces (ACMF) to the Wiltshire Regiment. The carvings are reputed to be the largest collection in Europe and each took around three months to make. At one time over twenty badges decorated the hillsides here but today there are less as some disappeared over time.

After the First World War the carvings were maintained by local workers, and some regimental associations also paid for the work to be done. In World War II the badges were allowed to grow over to avoid being landmarks for enemy aircraft. This, along with grazing cattle, caused some deterioration in their condition. The Fovant Home Guard restored them after the war and formed an Old Comrades Association, later becoming the Fovant Badges Society.

Today the badges are restored and maintained for all to see and require a constant effort to preserve them. They are etched into the countryside and are a unique reminder of the men who went to war in 1914–18.

THE BASICS

Distance: 6 miles / 9.5km

Gradient: Some inclines but mainly flat. A steep descent at the end.

Severity: Easy

Approx Time: 3–4 hrs

Stiles: Two and one kissing gate

Maps: OS Explorer 118 (Shaftesbury & Cranborne Chase)

Path description: Some mud tracks, fields and paths

Start point: Fovant Church. (GR ST 996295)

Parking: By Fovant Church. (SP3 5LA)

Dog friendly: Suitable for dogs but keep on a lead near farmland and around the A30

Public toilets: None

Nearest food: The Village Shop at the entrance to Fovant has snacks and is open daily. The nearest pub is a short drive away at The Compasses Inn, Lower Chicksgrove, SP3 6NB

FOVANT WALK

1. Park your car beside Fovant Church. Before starting the walk, visit 13th-century St George's Church and the war graves in the cemetery. Several Australian and Commonwealth servicemen are buried here. The church lectern is dedicated to servicemen who died in Fovant during World War I.

2. Walk back up the lane to the crossroads and turn left. About 100 yards up the road turn right down a bridleway. This path can be muddy. The bridleway climbs around 100 feet as it winds to the right through the north-eastern end of Dean Copse. After the copse there are lovely views across the village. When the path forks, take the right-hand path.

3. Follow the track between fields as the crest of the incline is reached, revealing the first glimpse of the Fovant Badges to the left. Continue along the track to the A30. Cross the road and take the lane signposted Bishopstoke. As the road turns to the right there is a small parking lay-by. Take the gate on the left. Follow the ridge path upwards. There are lovely views across the valley and glimpses of some of the badges. Keep to the right and continue along this track until you come to a gate and stile.

4. Take the track to the left along the Ridgeway with trees on either side. At the stile on the left, climb over it but not before looking to the right at the splendid valley view of Sheep Wash and Gurston Holes.

5. Walk across the field keeping the Iron Age hill fort on the left. This is Chiselbury Fort where archaeological digs have also uncovered Bronze Age and Roman remains. Walk around the hill fort until you are opposite the gate/stile into the field. Watch for the buildings in the distance to line up as in the photograph with the transit line marked (see page 12). At roughly that point start to walk away from the hill fort, looking out for a footway marker post. The route at this point is vague as the marker post won't be visible if you are too close to the fort. If you miss the marker post AND the transit you will arrive at some fencing. Do not attempt to walk down the hill at this point unless you know the area very well. RETRACE YOUR STEPS as you are above disused pit workings. They are safely fenced off at the time of writing but this cannot be guaranteed. Take care walking down this path as it is steep and winding and can be muddy.

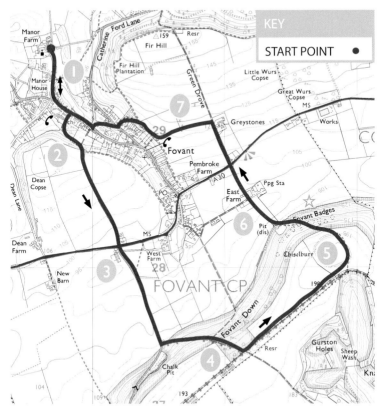

6. At the bottom of the hill turn right up the footpath and straight through East Farm towards the A30. At the road junction a good viewpoint of the Fovant Badges is 150 yards to the right in a lay-by. Take care when crossing this road as it is very busy.

7. After the viewpoint diversion return to the junction of Green Drove (opposite East Farm) on the A30. Turn right up Green Drove, heading uphill. In World War I this was the site of a 600-bed hospital. Shortly after passing some residential and farm buildings on the right, look for a large gap in the hedges. Follow the north side of the hedge. On the left a footpath leads through a field. Take the path along the edge of the field to a kissing gate in the corner. A track to the right leads down into Fovant village. The streams run through the village and at one time had watercress beds. Take the path ahead on Mill Lane. At the bottom end of Mill Lane turn right onto Tisbury Road. Follow Tisbury Road for 350 yards to Church Lane and head to the crossroads. Turn right towards the church and the end of the walk.

OLD SARUM

THIS WALK LEADS AROUND THE ANCIENT RUINS OF OLD SARUM AND THROUGH THE SURROUNDING COUNTRYSIDE ON THE OUTSKIRTS OF SALISBURY. OLD SARUM IS A UNIQUE PART OF ENGLISH HISTORY AND HERITAGE AND HAS A CASTLE AND CATHEDRAL COMBINED WITHIN A HUGE IRON AGE HILL FORT.

It is believed the earliest fortification here commenced in 400 BC and when the Romans arrived this area was known as Sorviodunum. In AD 522, following a Saxon battle victory here, the Kingdom of Wessex was formed.

Old Sarum was transformed in 1070 when William the Conqueror decided to build a castle in the middle of the old hill fort. With towers, apartments and an inner set of fortifications the site was divided in two and surrounded by a large outer bailey. This magnificent site was selected to house a new cathedral which was built by Bishop Roger in the early 12th century.

Old Sarum did not remain an influential fortress for very long because in 1220 the cathedral was moved to Salisbury, a settlement in the valley below. Only a few people remained at Old Sarum, which quickly fell into ruin. The Rotten Borough of Old Sarum continued to elect members of parliament until 1832. Today, there are quiet meadows and footpaths around Old Sarum and the views from the ramparts are as memorable to walkers as they were to King John in the Magna Carta era and in the eighteenth century to Thomas Mudge as he designed the first Ordnance Survey maps.

THE BASICS

Distance: 2 miles / 3.4km

Gradient: Some inclines but mainly flat

Severity: Easy

Approx Time: 1 hr

Stiles: Three

Maps: OS Explorer 130 (Salisbury & Stonehenge)

Path description: Some mud tracks, fields, road and paths

Start point: Old Sarum Car park (GR SU 139327)

Parking: In the car park at Old Sarum (SP1 3SD)

Dog friendly: Suitable for dogs but keep on a lead near farmland

Public toilets: At the Old Sarum car park

Nearest food: The Old Castle Pub which is across the road from the Old Sarum car park entrance. Snacks are sold in the English Heritage shop

OLD SARUM WALK

1. Walk from the car park back down the hill to the cross hatching on the bend. Go through the gate in the corner. Follow the path. Ahead are some lovely views of Salisbury and the cathedral. The Old Sarum ramparts and moat are to the right.

2. The path slopes gently down to a junction in the track. Take the left-hand path towards a farm. The site of the historic Parliament Tree is located in the field to the right and is where elections were once held for the Rotten Borough of Old Sarum. Before reaching the road turn right into a marked footpath. This path goes alongside a field with lovely views of the church at Stratford sub Castle. Cross into the next field via a stile. Walk across this field to the stile in the corner and go onto the road.

3. Ahead is the River Avon. Walk to the right and up the road past Dean's Farm. Follow this road uphill with good views across the countryside and farmland. The Old Sarum Castle ruins can be seen with the distinctive rounded shape covered by greenery.

4. As the edge of the castle appears ahead, take the footpath across a stile on the right. Follow the path around the castle as it climbs gently upwards giving some beautiful views of Salisbury and, on a good day, Salisbury Plain.

5. The path is part of the old rampart and curves around the former moat and fortress itself. Follow this around until you arrive at the main car park. Before completing the walk take time to climb up onto the outer walls of the castle in the car park to see a point marked to commemorate the time when Thomas Mudge looked out from Old Sarum in 1794 and commenced his work on the first Ordnance Survey maps.

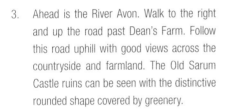

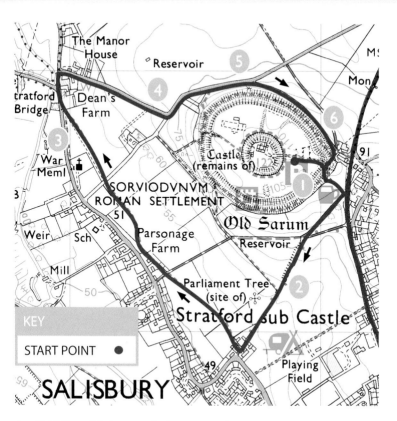

6. Finish the walk in the car park where you can also visit the inner bailey and cathedral and castle ruins at Old Sarum at an additional cost.

AVEBURY

This walk leads through the village of Avebury past mystical Silbury Hill to the ancient barrow of West Kennett. It returns via standing stones and circles to the picturesque village of Avebury where the stones can be seen up close.

Avebury is one of the most intriguing prehistoric areas in Britain and is the site of an ancient Neolithic henge monument. The village is almost enclosed within three stone circles, making it quite unique. Believed to have been formed between 2850 and 2200 BC the stones appear as an inner circle of stones surrounded by a huge ditch and with two further circles. They are linked by ancient avenues to Beckhampton and to Overton Hill, a mile away. The size of the structure suggests this area was a highly significant religious or political site in Neolithic times. During the Middle Ages many of the stones were associated with devil worship and paganism, with some being destroyed. In

Wiltshire the standing stones were made of sarsen, a hard sandstone rock found in the county and especially on the Marlborough Downs. Unlike other ancient sites visitors can walk up to the stones and touch them.

Silbury Hill is just outside the village and is a distinctive conical shape. It is the largest man-made mound in Europe and is thought to have been completed in 2400 BC. It covers around five acres and was so well constructed that there has been little erosion to it. The significance of Silbury Hill remains unknown but it is another of the mysterious structures in and around Avebury and a distinctive landmark. At West Kennet there is a long barrow believed to be an ancient burial chamber, and yet another mysterious feature on the landscape.

Alexander Keiller of the marmalade industry bought Avebury in 1925 and did much to excavate and restore the stone circles during the 1930s. Today there is a museum in his honour in the village which can be visited before or after the walk.

THE BASICS

Distance: 6 miles / 9.5km
Gradient: Some inclines but mainly flat
Severity: Easy
Approx time: 3 hrs
Stiles: Five
Maps: Explorer 157 (Marlborough and Savernake Forest)
Path description: Some mud tracks, fields, and paths
Start point: National Trust Car park. (GR SU 099696)
Parking: National trust Car Park (SN8 1RD Charge for parking unless NT member)
Dog friendly: Suitable for dogs but keep on a lead near farmland and around the A30
Public toilets: In Avebury village
Nearest food: Red Lion, Avebury; snacks in Avebury Village Shop

AVEBURY WALK

1. Begin at the National Trust car park just outside the village. Go back out of the car park entrance and to the right. A few yards up on the left is a footpath sign. Go through the gate and follow the path ahead.

2. As you continue to walk down this trail you will notice the distinctive shape of Silbury Hill on the right. Continue ahead along this track to a stile. Go through the stile. Walk to a second stile and cross it. Walk through the field to the main road.

3. At the main road cross over, taking care as it is busy. To the left is a marked footpath towards West Kennett. Take this path ahead.

4. This path curves to the left where there is a turn off to the left. If you plan to make a detour to the Long Barrow at West Kennett then follow the path ahead before returning to this trail. This is one of the most impressive Neolithic burial chambers in Europe and once held 50 people. Once back at the turn off go through two stiles and across farmland. The path curves to the right. At the end of the path take the turning to the left.

5. This track can be muddy and leads to the road and village of East Kennett. Go over the bridge to the left and take the footpath on the right. Walk along this farmland track to the end of the trail. Turn left.

6. Walk up this track to the road, which is busy with cars parked in the lay-by. In the field to the right are a number of standing stones. At the top of the track to the left is the Sanctuary and another of the stone circles. The origins of the Sanctuary are unknown but it may have been the burial place of a dignitary.

7. Cross the road and continue up the path named the Ridgeway. Ancient tumuli can be seen on the right. About half a mile (1km) up the Ridgeway at a junction with a footpath take the left-hand track. This leads past another ancient burial mound topped with trees. Continue along the trail past farmland and with beautiful views across the countryside to the road.

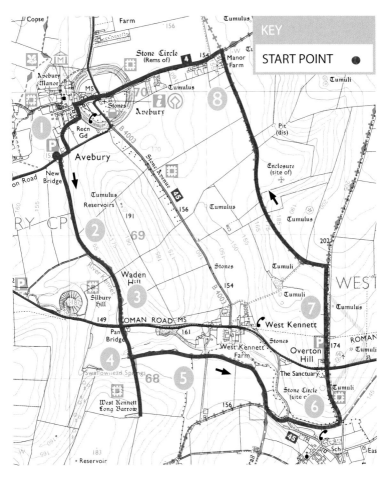

KEY

START POINT ●

8. At the farm junction with the road turn left. This road leads back into the village of Avebury where there are more stone circles, Avebury Manor and the Keiller Museum to enjoy.

BERWICK ST JAMES

BERWICK MEANS 'BARLEY FARM' IN THE SAXON LANGUAGE
AND THIS IS AGRICULTURAL COUNTRY CLOSE TO SALISBURY
PLAIN. THIS WALK TAKES YOU THROUGH FARMLAND
AND THE SCENIC VILLAGES OF BERWICK ST JAMES AND
WINTERBOURNE STOKE.

The oldest houses in this small village date from the 16th century, and there are several pretty cottages along the High Street. Many houses have histories attached and at one time several were the sites of shops and other businesses. The Berwick St James Farm Shop is on the site of a forge and the Old Post Office once sold all manner of items as well as stamps. There are standing or sarsen stones in the village and these are believed to have come from the altar stone at Stonehenge. The working mill at Berwick Bridge still pumps water to Berwick Hill Farm and there are pleasant walks close to the river. Berwick St James is also one of the best places to spot the great bustard, Wiltshire's county bird.

Great bustards all but disappeared from Wiltshire in the 19th century and the last one was actually shot at Berwick Hill Farm in 1871. It was stuffed and can be seen in Salisbury Museum. In 2004 great bustards were reintroduced to Salisbury Plain and there have been several hatchings of chicks. great bustards are unique in that they are unable to perch due to the absence of a hind claw. They live on the ground and are sometimes seen flying around Berwick St James. Hares can also be seen in this area as well as several species of wild flower.

THE BASICS

Distance: 5 miles / 8km

Gradient: Some inclines but mainly flat

Severity: Easy

Approx time: 3 hrs

Stiles: None

Maps: OS Explorer 130 (Salisbury & Stonehenge)

Path description: Some mud tracks, fields, road and paths

Start point: High Street, Berwick St James (GR SU 071392)

Parking: High Street, Berwick St James (SP3 4TP)

Dog friendly: Suitable for dogs but keep on a lead near farmland and A303

Public toilets: None en route but there are facilities for pub customers

Nearest food: The Boot Inn, Berwick St James (book at weekends); snacks and delicious local produce are available at Berwick St James Farm Shop. The Bell at Winterbourne Stoke

1. Start from the High Street in Berwick St James and walk towards Berwick Bridge. On the way stop at St James Church which has a Norman nave. The poet Edward Thomas likened the table tombs here to 'luggage left at a station'.

2. From the church walk down the road and at Berwick Bridge there is a watermill. Go over the bridge and walk straight ahead to a byway. Walk straight ahead up this lane. To the right are some ancient earthworks. The track leads gently uphill and past Druid's Head Wood. On reaching Druid's Head Farm turn left.

3. Take the track to the left and continue ahead. This is working farmland and at harvest time this track can get very busy with agricultural machinery. At Hope Down, take the path to the left. This is a field path with trees on the right. At the end of this track the path leads to a wooded area.

4. Take the path to the right and follow this around and past a large tree trunk. The path leads to a kissing gate and downhill along a narrow track past a thatched cottage.

5. Take the road to the right through the village of Winterbourne Stoke to the A303. At the junction turn left unless you plan to stop at the pub opposite; there are traffic lights to cross. This road is very busy and care should be taken with children and animals. Continue up the road past one footpath sign. At the second footpath sign which is beside a manor house take the path to the left.

6. Turn left down this footpath and continue past a house and through a field. This field path leads to another footpath in a field. Go through the gate and turn right. Continue along the path which runs beside a campsite and houses to a field.

7. At the field there is a path marked by the owner. Depending on the time of year it may be cut through crops or be defined on the grass. Continue through the field on the path

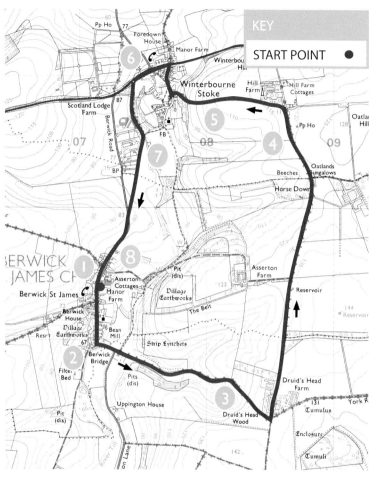

towards the fence on the right where there is a kissing gate. Go through the kissing gate and turn left.

8. Continue straight down this road which leads to Berwick St James and the High Street. The Boot Inn is on the left-hand side.

STEEPLE ASHTON

This walk starts in the beautiful village of Steeple Ashton and heads out across the countryside to Keevil. It passes the old Keevil Airfield before returning to Steeple Ashton. The picturesque village of Steeple Ashton is quintessentially English with thatched cottages, beautiful gardens and a village green. It lacks the tourists that crowd many other Wiltshire villages and is a thriving rural community.

On the village green is a blind house, which characterises a number of towns and villages in Wiltshire. Blind houses were village prisons and were constructed with no windows and with very claustrophobic conditions. They were typically used to lock up drunk and disorderly people in the 18th century and the only ventilation came from grilles in the wall.

Keevil is a small village that grew up around the cloth industry. Most houses are on Main Street and St Laurence Church has many box graves of wealthy clothiers. Keevil Airfield played a significant role in the Second World War and has been a large part of the community here. This is where many spitfires and gliders departed for the D-Day landings in 1944 and later for Operation Market Garden at Arnhem. The airfield is occasionally used by the Royal Air Force today and has a glider club.

THE BASICS

Distance: 4 miles / 7km

Gradient: Mostly flat

Severity: Easy

Approx time: 3 hrs

Stiles: Five and one kissing gate

Maps: OS Explorer 143 (Warminster & Trowbridge)

Path description: Some mud tracks, fields, and paths

Start point: Main Street, Steeple Ashton (GR ST 907567)

Parking: Main Street, Steeple Ashton (BA14 6EU)

Dog friendly: Suitable for dogs but keep on a lead near farmland

Public toilets: None on the walk but there are toilets for pub customers

Nearest food: The Village Shop in Steeple Ashton serves coffees and snacks. The Longs Arms is a popular pub serving meals

STEEPLE ASHTON WALK

1. Start on the village high street and walk past the green and blind house to the church. St Mary the Virgin Church has very distinctive and ornate architecture on the roof. To the left of the church is a public footpath. Walk along this track until you come to a kissing gate on the right-hand side.

2. Go through the gate and walk through the field, which can be muddy. Cross through a gate to a second field. At this field there is a gate leading to a bridge over a stream. Follow the track ahead along the field. When you reach a 'junction' in the path go right. Walk over towards the right through a path that leads to a field. Walk through the field and to another field. There are lovely views of the villages from here.

3. On the left-hand side is a stile leading to common ground meadowland. Go through this meadow and head for the church. Walk through the churchyard and through the gate below the church. At the end of the path and at the school turn right.

4. Carry on down the Main Street in Keevil past timbered houses and a high pavement. Continue to the corner of the road.

5. Turn right up a small road with houses on either side. This leads to a grassy trail which is tree-lined in places. On the left-hand side is Keevil Airfield and the original buildings can be seen in the distance. Gliders can often be seen taking off and landing. Stay on the path until there is a stile on the left. Go through the stile into a field which was once a runway. Walk towards the gate and go through it.

6. Ahead is an office building. To the left is an open-sided barn and behind this is a marked stile. Cross the stile into the field and continue walking to another stile.

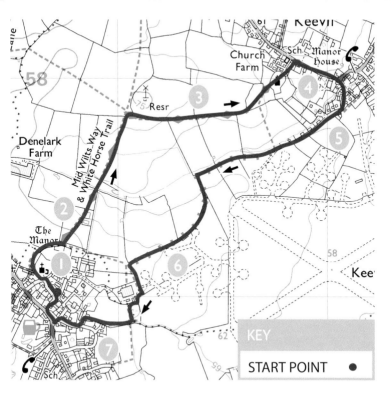

KEY

START POINT ●

Cross this into a field and walk to the bottom left-hand corner. There is a stile leading to a footpath.

7. Cross the stile and continue along the footpath to the right. This leads past houses. Turn left and follow the road around to the right. This leads past beautiful old timbered houses back into the village green and the blind house with the pub and village shop opposite.

MERE

THE SMALL HISTORIC TOWN OF MERE AND THE SURROUNDING DOWNS ARE VERY SCENIC FOR WALKING. THIS WALK TAKES IN THE TOWN, THE DISTINCTIVE MERE DOWNS AND TWO ANCIENT CASTLES, AND LOOPS ROUND IN A HORSESHOE.

Mere Castle dominates the town. It was built by Richard, Earl of Cornwall in 1253 but gradually fell into disrepair. Much of the stone was used to build local houses and there are some wonderful views from the top.

There is evidence to suggest that farming was going on in and around Mere in Neolithic times and the ancient camp on White Sheet Hill has burial barrows dating back 2,000 years. The long track at the north of Mere Down once connected camps, later becoming a drovers' path. Today it is a walking trail connecting sections of Mere Down and has historic milestones along the route from its days as a turnpike road in the 1750s. One of the most distinctive sights on Mere Down is the strip lynchets on steep slopes used for farming. They date from prehistoric and medieval times as a way of cultivating the land. Today their patterns define the landscape on Mere Down, giving the views a unique feature on this walk.

THE BASICS

Distance: 5 miles / 8km

Gradient: There is a steep ascent at the start of Mere Down and also at Mere Castle

Severity: Easy with two steep ascents

Approx time: 3 hrs

Stiles: Three stiles at Mere Castle and there are steps leading to the summit

Maps: OS Explorer 143 (Warminster & Trowbridge)

Path description: Footpaths, road and lanes

Start point: Salisbury Street Car Park, Mere (GR ST 814323)

Parking: Salisbury Street Car Park, Mere (BA12 6HB)

Dog friendly: Suitable for dogs but keep on a lead near farmland and A303

Public toilets: At Salisbury Street Car Park

Nearest food: Several pubs and cafes in Mere. The Walnut Tree serves food all day, The Angel Tea Rooms is also good for light snacks and refreshments

MERE WALK

1. Park in the main car park in Mere. Turn right and continue up the road. At the junction there is a wine merchant's shop straight ahead. Take the fork to the left and continue up this road past the fire station and police station.

2. Ahead is the road bridge. To the left of the arch is a marked footpath. Take this path up to a gate and go through it. Turn right and walk a short distance along this path to a stile on the right. Cross the stile and take the path to the left.

3. Continue along this path with views of Mere on the left. The path leads steeply uphill to a stile. Cross the stile into a field with a path to the left-hand side. This path leads around the fields and has views across the landscape with the strip lynchets and distinctive curves in the land.

4. Walk along this path until you reach a stile. This is the historic drovers' path. Turn left. Just a short distance on the left is a milestone dating from 1750. Pass one footpath and at the second footpath sign on the left, go through the gate and cross the field.

5. Keep to the path which leads towards a reservoir within the ruins of White Sheet Castle and then turns to the left skirting the fence. This was a Neolithic settlement and hill fort.

6. The path forks to the right once the fence ends. Take this path and walk down across a ridge with views across Mere Downs on either side. Continue walking downhill and at a fork in the path keep to the left-hand track straight ahead.

7. The path continues downhill, eventually leading to the right and a gate. Walk through the gate and carry on straight ahead past a farmhouse to the road.

8. Turn left at the road and continue over the bridge with the noisy A303 below.

9. This road leads into Mere. About 100 yards up on the right is a footpath to Mere Castle. Walk up the wooded track to some steps and climb them to a grassy path.

10. Take the upper right-hand path which circles the base of the castle and has views across Mere Down. On the left is a track leading upwards and to the left. Take this

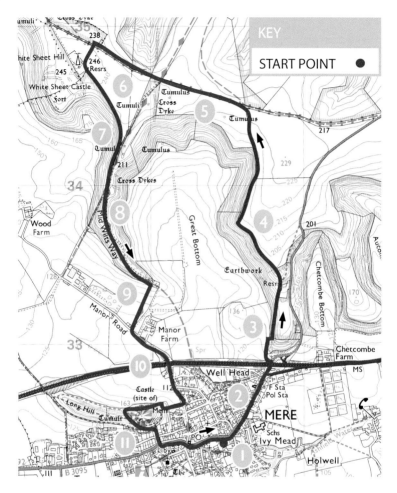

path which leads to the castle summit. Take a few moments to enjoy the views across Mere and the Downs, and see the walk you have just completed.

11. Take the path downwards and to the left which leads down past a playground and along a footpath to the town centre where the walk finishes. There are opportunities to enjoy a visit to Mere Museum or visit the shops and local pubs.

LANGLEY BURRELL

"To the memory of the worthy Maud Heath of Langley Burrell, widow, who in the year of grace 1474 for the good of travellers did in charity bestow in land and houses about eight pounds a year for ever to be laid out on the highways and causey leading from Wick Hill to Chippenham Clift. This pillar was set up by the feoffees in 1698. Injure me not."

The writing on the memorial in Langley Burrell is a reminder of the extraordinary legacy of the 15th-century widow who sold eggs and butter in Chippenham. She frequently had to wade through floodwater from the River Avon to get to market but Maud Heath had a vision. When she died in 1474 she left a legacy of land and the sum of eight pounds a year so that a causeway across the flood plain could be built, saving her fellow villagers and market traders from wading through mud and floodwater for generations to come. The four-and-a-half-mile path of cobblestones can still be seen in parts today. In 1811 the Maud Heath Trustees constructed a magnificent 64-arch causeway at Kellaways just outside Langley Burrell and over the floodplain.

Langley Burrell was also home to the diarist Francis Kilvert, who lived at the vicarage. The scenery surrounding Langley Burrell inspired much of his writing. This walk takes in the famous Maud Heath Causeway as well as the scenic footpaths around the Langley Burrell of Francis Kilvert. At nearby Bremhill a monument to Maud Heath stands in a field overlooking the lanes and countryside where she would have walked. This can be visited after the walk.

THE BASICS

Distance: 2½ miles / 4km

Gradient: Mainly flat

Severity: Easy

Approx time: 2 hrs

Stiles: One

Maps: OS Explorer 156 (Chippenham & Bradford on Avon)

Path description: Pavement, the causeway, fields and footpaths

Start point: Langley Tap Pub, Langley Burrell (GR ST 933752)

Parking: On the main street in the village, take care not to obstruct gateways (SN15 4LQ)

Dog friendly: Suitable for dogs but keep on a lead near farmland.

Public toilets: None. Toilets are available for pub customers at the Langley Tap

LANGLEY BURRELL WALK

1. Start at the Langley Tap pub and turn right, walking down the road which is part of the original causeway. Soon several pieces of historic cobblestone paving will be seen along the route. At the junction turn right past a red brick Victorian house.

2. Continue down this road to the railway tunnel and the distinctive 64 arches of Maud Heath's Causeway. The memorial to Maud Heath is also in this area and worth stopping to read. It was erected in 1698 in remembrance of this remarkable woman. Ahead is the small church of St Giles. Just after the chapel on the right-hand side is a black post marking a stile.

3. Climb over the stile and onto the footpath which leads through a field to an opening. Go through this opening and follow the track around the field and along the river. Ahead is a small bridge across the River Avon. Cross the bridge into the next field.

4. Walk along the track to the right with the river also on your right past a World War II pillbox. Continue along the river path past some trees. This was very much the scenery that Francis Kilvert enjoyed in this area and inspired his writing. On the right is a gate leading to a lane. Continue up this lane to a junction with a bridleway.

5. Turn right and continue along the bridleway taking the first left to the railway bridge. Walk up the footpath past houses. At the junction with the road turn left onto the causeway and the Langley Tap is on the left-hand side. An option at the end of this walk is to drive over to nearby Bremhill to see the large monument to Maud Heath on Wick Hill. The views from this structure are magnificent and the farm shop next door sells eggs, just like Maud Heath did.

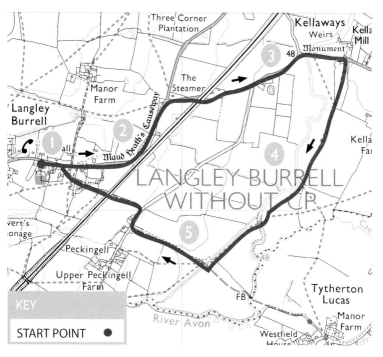

KEY

START POINT ●

CORSHAM

CORSHAM IS A LOVELY MARKET TOWN IN WEST WILTSHIRE WITH BATH STONE BUILDINGS AND 17TH-CENTURY FLEMISH HOMES AS WELL AS SOME HISTORIC PUBS AND DISTINCTIVE ALMSHOUSES.

There are even peacocks in the streets in this town that grew up around the wool trade and was on the historic coaching route to London. Corsham Court is on the edge of the town and its splendid park makes a lovely walk.

The records for Corsham Court date back to AD 985, when the site was a summer palace for the kings of Wessex. Richard Plantagenet, the son of King John, was also associated with Corsham and held the town until the end of the 13th century. It then became a dowry for the queens of England until Elizabeth I granted a lease to one of her subjects. In 1582 Thomas Smythe built a fine house on the parkland. When Paul Methuen took over the house in 1747 a lot of developments took place in the classical style including Palladian designs to the north front, and this was further restored over the next few hundred years. In 1760 Capability Brown designed the grounds and parkland at Corsham Court.

The Corsham Estate consists of 2,500 acres of farmland and includes 100 cottages and several farms. There are over 2,000 sheep on the land and Corsham Park is known for its extensive woodland. Today Corsham Court is open to the public and is part of the heritage of the town. It is renowned for its collection of paintings which were largely amassed by Sir Paul Methuen. Amongst the more well-known works is The Betrayal of Christ by Sir Anthony Van Dyck. The walk takes in Corsham Park and the countryside within the Corsham Estate, returning to the town.

THE BASICS

Distance: 4 miles / 7.5km

Gradient: Mainly flat with a slight incline on the road

Severity: Easy

Approx time: 3 hrs

Stiles: Five

Maps: OS Explorer 156 (Chippenham & Bradford on Avon)

Path description: Paths, fields, road

Start point: Car park next to football ground on Lacock Road (GR ST 880702)

Parking: Car park next to football ground on Lacock Road (SN13 9HS) there is also a car park in Corsham town centre

Dog friendly: Yes, but keep dogs on leads near livestock

Public toilets: In Corsham town centre

Nearest food: Corsham Court cafe, and several pubs and cafes in Corsham

1. Park in the free car park for Corsham Park, which is located next to the football ground. Go out of the car park and cross the road where there is a gap in the estate stone wall. Once you reach the path with Corsham Lake in front of you turn right.

2. The path leads past horse chestnut trees and at the end of the track go through the gate ahead. To the right is a narrow footpath which is marked. Walk down this track to a stile.

3. Cross the stile into a field and walk across it to another stile which leads onto a narrow road.

4. Turn left and carry on up this road past farm houses. Just after a small stream there is a turning to the right. Follow this trail to the fields and climb over the stile.

5. Walk to the far left corner to a stile and climb over it. Ahead is a stile in the top right corner of the field. Cross this and continue up a lane to the road.

6. On the road continue to the junction. Turn left and continue walking uphill.

7. At the junction with the busy road look for the entrance to Corsham Park on the left. Go into the park keeping to the footpath. There are usually sheep in this part of the park so any dogs should be kept on a lead.

8. Take the footpath to the right and head for a line of oak trees. Once you reach the trees there is a path to the left.

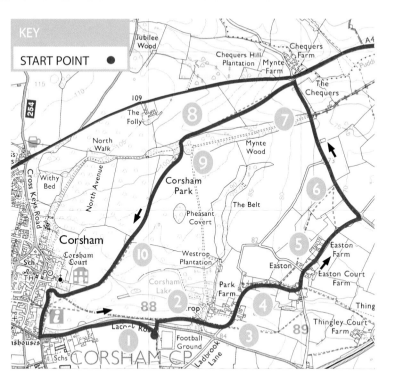

9. Take this path through woodland to the wider park. Keep to the right and walk along a long trail through Corsham Park. The lake is on the left. Ahead are views of Corsham Court. The church of St Bartholomew is on the right-hand side. Corsham Court also has a tea room within the park.

10. At the end of the trail turn left and continue to the park gates. Go out onto the road and turn left, continuing up the road to the car park. Alternatively head into the town centre to see more of the shops, cafes and historic buildings.

BIDDESTONE

LOCATED IN THE WILTSHIRE COTSWOLDS, BIDDESTONE IS A QUIET AND QUINTESSENTIALLY BEAUTIFUL VILLAGE BUT WITHOUT THE CROWDS OF TOURISTS SEEN ELSEWHERE IN THIS AREA. IT IS AN AREA KNOWN FOR ITS WOOL, FARMING AND GRAIN MILLS.

The walk leads through Biddestone and then out into the surrounding countryside through the Weavern Woods and back to the village green. Biddestone Green is characterised by its delightful duck pond and Cotswold style houses and historic architecture. The ducks are reputed to be the best fed in Wiltshire.

Biddestone dates back to Saxon times but most buildings here are from the late 18th century. One of the buildings, known locally as The Barracks, is reputed to have accommodated Parliamentarian troops during the English Civil War, and before they destroyed nearby Slaughterford Church. On the Green is a 16th-

century house that was once a clothier's factory. In Cuttle Street several cottages can be seen which probably date to the 16th century. Around Biddestone there are Cotswold slab stiles, typical of the area.

The village pump sits under a tiled roof and adds to Biddestone's charm. It is one of four structures that were designed by W.H. Poynder of Hartnam Park. The Norman church of St Nicholas has an unusual bell turret dating from the 13th century and a Maltese cross over the porch.

The village makes a good base for long and short walks around the countryside and has two pubs which are popular with locals and visitors. More recently Biddestone has been the location for the TV adaptation of the Agatha Raisin crime books.

THE BASICS

Distance: 4 miles / 7km

Gradient: A steep downhill at the beginning with a slight gradient in the woods and leading back to Biddestone

Severity: Easy

Approx time: 3 hrs

Stiles: None

Maps: OS Explorer 156 (Chippenham & Bradford on Avon)

Path description: Road, tracks, and woodland path that can get muddy

Start point: Village green, Biddestone (GR ST 863735)

Parking: Village green, Biddestone (SN14 7DG)

Dog friendly: Yes, but keep on a lead near livestock and the ducks

Public toilets: On The Butts in Biddestone

Nearest food: Two pubs in the village. The White Horse and the Biddestone Arms serve food. It is advisable to book a table at weekends as they can get really busy

BIDDESTONE WALK

1. Park on the main street in Biddestone beside the village green. Take care not to obstruct any entrances to houses. Walk up the street towards the red phone box in the street called The Butts. On the right-hand side is the historic water pump within its distinctive shelter.

2. Continue walking up the road and on the right is St Nicholas' Church and some beautiful cottages and gardens. Further down the road is a mill. The views here open out onto fields sloping downhill and woodlands.

3. Walk down the steep hill at Weavern Lane which is a 1 in 20 gradient. At the end of this track turn left into the wooded path and walk through the woods.

4. This track can be muddy, especially in wet weather. In spring the sides of this path are carpeted with bluebells, and it leads through the trees with farmland on either side. The woodland track continues slightly uphill towards a road. Once the road is reached turn left.

5. Continue walking up the narrow lane and at the junction with another road, turn left.

6. Continue up this road past a few cottages and follow the road back into Biddestone village.

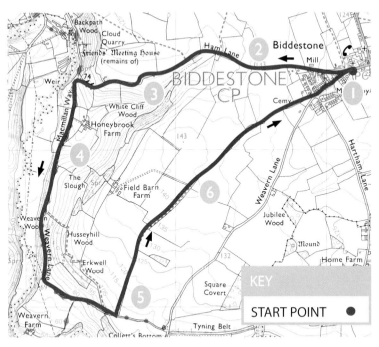

KEY

START POINT ●

DOWNTON

The small village of Downton gets visitors looking for the famous TV series these days, but this is not the location for Downton Abbey. There are, however, many interesting things to see on a walk around the village here and visitors can learn about the history of the area.

Downton is part of an Ancient Borough and lies on the River Avon. The walk leads through the village and out to the weirs and water meadows surrounding Downton. Whilst walking there are visible traces of the historic ways in which these water meadows were managed. Drowners worked in partnership with shepherds and agricultural workers on a highly specialised form of irrigation on the chalkland downs in Wiltshire. Long drainage channels cut into the meadows allowed water in and this resulted in more grass being grown for animals as well as bigger hay crops. The dung from the sheep aided in fertilising the soil. These water meadows are also a habitat for local wildlife.

Downton Moot is an 18th-century garden that was created out of the ruins of a 12th-century Norman earthwork castle. These grounds have several trails and an amphitheatre which make a pleasant end to the walk. Downton is also known for its annual Cuckoo Fair which is held to welcome in the spring.

NOTE: local residents showed us pictures of the water meadows in full flood and if there has been substantial rainfall and flooding in this area, this walk may not be passable. Also this route may not be very suitable for dogs unless on a lead due to livestock and particularly the fast-flowing river and weirs. For the same reason, children should also be observed and supervised closely on this walk.

THE BASICS

Distance: 4 miles / 6km
Gradient: Mainly flat
Severity: Easy but pay attention to uneven channels underfoot on the water meadows
Approx time: 2–3 hrs
Stiles: Three
Maps: OS Explorer 130 (Salisbury & Stonehenge)
Path description: Road, path, water meadow, farm track
Start point: Downton Moot Car Park (GR SU 181213)
Parking: Downton Moot Car park, Moot Lane, Downton (SP5 3JP)
Dog friendly: On leads throughout
Public toilets: At the park in Downton
Nearest food: Downton has two pubs (The Wooden Spoon and The White Horse). The Borough Café also serves light meals and snacks

DOWNTON WALK

1. The walk commences from the Downton
   Moot car park on Moot Lane. From the
   car park turn left and walk down to the
   main street. At the crossroads continue
   straight ahead to Barford Lane.

2. Walk up this road past houses and past a
   Catholic church. Shortly after the church
   the road turns to the right but take the
   track to the left marked fisheries. Follow
   this trail down to a farm track and through
   grass parkland.

3. On reaching a house take the stile to the
   right and follow the trail around to the
   left. This goes past a disused chapel, a
   mill and some footbridges. Follow the car
   park to the end of the trail and take the
   footbridge across the River Avon.

4. Walk onwards on a wooden trailway
   through the crossings on the weir and
   waterfall. Cross the bridge and follow
   the path around to the right and straight
   ahead. This leads to a field. Take the path
   to the top left corner and cross the stile.

5. Cross the stile into the field and walk
   down to the middle of the hedge. Cross
   another stile. There are channels here for drainage of the water meadows. Cross
   the field to another stile. Turn left and continue walking along a track beside a
   river. Follow the concrete road down past the Avon.

6. On reaching a house turn left, crossing a bridge. Walk back to Downton over the
   water meadows taking care underfoot as some of the channels and brickwork
   make the ground uneven underfoot. At the town edge of the water meadow there
   is a path to the main street. The tannery building is close by, which was once a
   major industry in the village.

7. By turning left the road leads past a pub and on to Downton Moot and the car
   park. On the right-hand side is a café and pub as well as shops and a park.

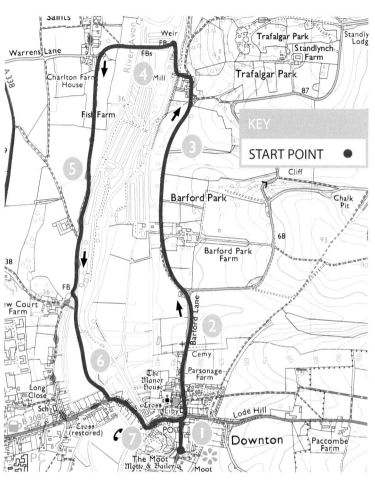

KEY

START POINT ●

GREAT BEDWYN

GREAT BEDWYN IS A QUIET VILLAGE ON THE KENNET AND AVON CANAL AND IS CHARACTERISED BY ITS DELIGHTFUL FLINT COTTAGES. THE CANAL IS THE MAIN REASON TO VISIT GREAT BEDWYN AND JOINING THE TWO RIVERS IN THIS WAY WAS FIRST PROPOSED IN 1788 AND COMPLETED IN 1810.

The canal was a busy thoroughfare and transported goods from the Somerset coalfield, iron, slate and timber, and was a link between London and Bath for luxury merchandise. The canals operated for 40 years until the advent of the railways when they went into decline. Today they are frequented by walkers, naturalists and narrowboat owners.

The walk takes in the Kennet and Avon Canal leading to Little Bedwyn and then onward to a deserted chapel and the hamlet of Chisbury before returning to Great Bedwyn via woodlands. In Great Bedwyn the old stonemason's shop is worth a stop to read the engravings adorning the walls that were made by local workers. These are outside the post office and some are amusing to read and quite unique.

THE BASICS

Distance: 5 miles / 8km

Gradient: Some inclines but mainly flat along the towpath

Severity: Easy

Approx time: 3 hrs

Stiles: None

Maps: OS Explorer 157 (Marlborough & Savernake Forest)

Path description: Canal path, road, footpaths, fields

Start point: Great Bedwyn Station (GR SU 278645)

Parking: On the street in Great Bedwyn (SN8 3NU)

Dog friendly: Suitable for dogs but keep on a lead near farmland

Public toilets: none

Nearest food: There is a post office for snacks, and the Three Tuns pub serves meals

GREAT BEDWYN WALK

1. The walk starts at Great Bedwyn railway station. On leaving the station proceed over the railway bridge to the left. Cross the second bridge and turn immediately right to a parking area beside the canal.

2. Turn right under the tunnel and carry on walking down the towpath. There are lots of barges here, some being people's homes. Walk past one lock. Go past the next lock (Lock 66).

3. At the next lock cross the footbridge to the hamlet of Little Bedwyn. Walk over to the church, which has an exquisite millennium painting of the village with every house and field, created by one of the parishioners.

4. Go back out onto the road and turn right up the hill. This road twists and turns uphill. At the sign for Chisbury Chapel turn left and follow a track to this 13th-century building. This has a splendid thatched roof and was taken out of use in 1547, spending 300 years being used as a barn.

5. Go back out onto the road and continue left up the hill which skirts the old Chisbury Hill fort. At a junction with the road turn right towards Chisbury village.

6. Turn left by the phone box into the village and continue up the road past houses and some woodland. On the left is a metal farm gate. Go through this gate into a field where there are hides. Head for the hide at the left-hand corner and then aim for the trees ahead.

7. In the woods to the left is a gate. Go through this and carry straight through the woods past a small house on the right. Carry on through the woods to a clearing.

8. Take the track ahead which goes to the left and downhill. As you come out of the wood you will see a phone mast as a landmark. At the clearing you will be in a field.

9. Turn right and walk along the edge of the field. At the junction with the road, turn left. Continue down this road to arrive back in Great Bedwyn.

CRICKLADE

KNOWN AS THE FIRST TOWN ON THE RIVER THAMES, CRICKLADE IS FULL OF HISTORY AND DELIGHTFUL BUILDINGS. IT WAS BUILT BY ALFRED THE GREAT AS A DEFENCE AGAINST THE DANES AND AT ONE TIME WAS CONSIDERED SO STRATEGICALLY IMPORTANT THAT IT MINTED ITS OWN COINS.

A walk through Cricklade passes many delightful old cottages and buildings, with small footbridges to houses on the High Street and the Thames trickling underneath. Cricklade is on the National Thames Trail Footpath leading to London and this walk takes in the town and North Meadow National Nature Reserve.

The North Meadow National Nature Reserve is home to several species of wild flower and fauna including reed bunting and skylarks. In particular it is the home to the largest collection in the UK of wild snake's head fritillary, which flowers in April and early May. It is believed that up to 80 per cent of the species in the UK grows in this reserve.

The meadow is located between the Churn and Thames rivers and the habitat needed for these flowers is caused by winter flooding. Many towns had a meadow like this but the majority have disappeared for building. Cricklade's has remained thanks to an ancient Saxon system of town governance called the Court Leet.

THE BASICS

Distance: 3 miles / 5km

Gradient: Mostly flat

Severity: Easy

Approx time: 2 hrs

Stiles: None

Maps: OS Explorer 169 (Cirencester & Swindon)

Path description: Road, footpath, meadow

Start point: Cricklade Car Park, High Street, Cricklade (GR SU 099936)

Parking: Cricklade Car Park, High Street, Cricklade (SN6 6AY)

Dog friendly: Suitable for dogs but keep on a lead near farmland

Public toilets: At the car park in Cricklade

Nearest food: Cricklade has several cafes and pubs on the High Street. The White Hart serves meals throughout the day

1. The walk starts at the car park entrance on High Street. Turn left and walk up the wide High Street with shops, cafes and floral displays. On the left is the Catholic church which was restored in Victorian times but has a history dating back to Saxon and medieval times. Continue up the High Street to the sign for the North Wall.

2. The North Wall marks the historic town boundary and the Thames. On the left is the historic Prior House which was a resting place for pilgrims. The origins date from beyond the 12th century and a medieval stank or dam ran alongside the tannery yard here at one time which was used in the glove-making industry. Continue over the bridge crossing the River Thames. On the left take the footpath into North Meadow National Nature Reserve.

3. Continue on the marked path across the meadow. The path curves around to follow a trail beside the river. Depending on the time of year there are displays of wild flowers here as well as bird sightings.

4. Walk through to a larger meadow and walk along the path to the left of the field. Pass two footbridges on the left. At the edge of the meadow go up the steps to a high footbridge and cross this to a gate.

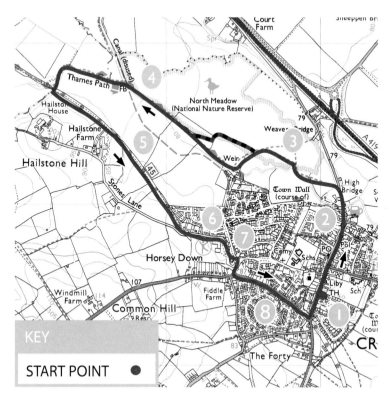

KEY

START POINT ●

5. Go through the gate and cross the field towards some farm buildings. At the gate turn left and continue walking down the Thames Cycle Path.

6. Walk under the old railway bridge. This leads back into the town eventually. Continue along this trail following the road around and past the leisure centre. Continue walking to the roundabout and turn left.

7. Walk up this road and at the bus shelter cross over and use the footpath running alongside the houses. Follow this road to the end as it emerges onto a roundabout. Turn left into the town centre.

8. Walk up the high street past the high pavements and bridges over the River Thames. Several houses have decorative steps with snake's head fritillaries on them. The walk ends at the main car park in Cricklade.

BARBURY CASTLE

Perched on the top of the Marlborough Downs, Barbury Castle has magnificent views across the Wiltshire countryside and is crossed by the famous Ridgeway National Trail. This 12-acre hill fort remains steep and imposing on the landscape, even after 2,000 years of erosion.

It commands views at the head of the valley of the River Og and thus defended the approaches to Wessex from the north along with the hill fort at nearby Liddington Hill.

In AD 556 the Battle of Beranburh was fought here as the Saxons invaded Wiltshire. Today the perimeter and surrounding landscape make an excellent walk to appreciate the views as well as the history. There is evidence of the Celtic field management or lynchet system here too with strips ploughed closely into the hills.

The area around Barbury Castle has also inspired writers including some of Wiltshire's finest such as Alfred Williams, who wrote a series of poems entitled 'About Wiltshire'. At the end of this walk and close to Barbury Castle are sarsen stone memorials to Alfred Williams and Richard Jefferies, who spent much of their time here.

The memorial to Alfred Williams particularly encapsulates his love of the Marlborough Downs with the quotation:

"Still to find and still to follow
Joy in every hill and hollow
Company in solitude."

THE BASICS

Distance: 4 miles / 7km

Gradient: Short climb to the hill fort ridge, uphill onto the ridge, & the final uphill walk

Severity: Easy

Approx time: 3 hrs

Stiles: None

Maps: OS Explorer 169 (Cirencester & Swindon) 157 (Marlborough & Savernake)

Path description: Mainly footpaths and a field

Start point: Car park at Barbury Castle (GR SU 156761)

Parking: Car park, Barbury Castle (nearest SN4 0QH)

Dog friendly: Suitable for dogs but keep on a lead near farmland and shooting school

Public toilets: Car park, Barbury Castle

Nearest food: None at the castle itself but there are some excellent picnic spots with a view. The nearest pub with food is the Calley Arms, Hodson, SN4 0QG

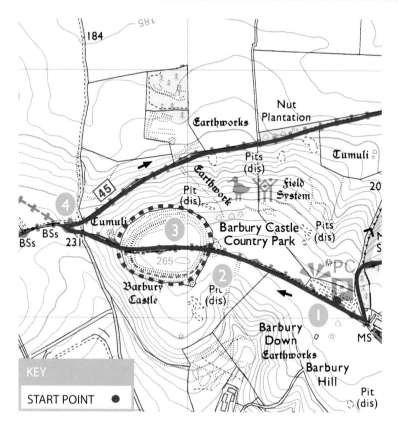

KEY

START POINT ●

1. This walk begins in the car park at Barbury Castle. Walk over to the footpath to the rear of the public toilets and go through the gate.

2. Walk through the country park towards the hill fort and walk through another gate. There are sweeping views of the Wiltshire countryside from here.

3. Once at the hill fort climb to the upper ridge and walk around the perimeter. The views are splendid and it is an opportunity to appreciate the size of this ancient monument. Once the perimeter has been walked then walk straight through the hill fort. This was once a wooden fortress and had sarsen stones as defences.

4. At the gate turn right. Carry on down the track for 100 yards and then take a right turn into a footpath. Walk down this trail. There is a hazelnut plantation further down the path and this is also where the strip lynchets can be seen in the hillside and along the edge of the fort.

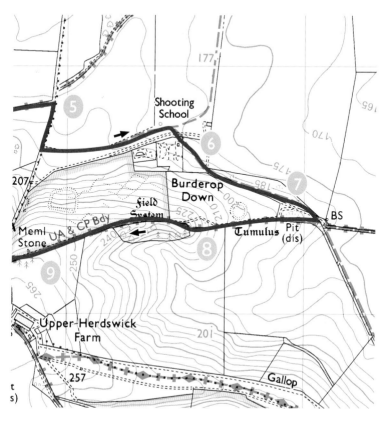

5. At the junction of the path with the road turn right. Take the public bridleway on the left which is well marked. This leads through a field. Alternatively, if you want to finish the walk at this point then simply walk back up the hill to the car park.

6. Walk through the marked path in the field. This is close to a shooting school which has protective barriers in place and is a major reason for keeping to the marked trails. At the end of the trail pass the shooting school, walking towards a shed. Turn right and follow the path uphill.

7. Take the left-hand path through a tree-lined track. At the end of this track take a sharp right turn. Walk up the trail and follow the path around and uphill across

the ridge. The views from the ridge summit are worth the climb.

8. Continue over the ridge passing the shooting school from above. Ahead are the sarsen stone memorials to Richard Jefferies and Alfred Williams, who so enjoyed these views. At the end of the track turn left and walk uphill for 100 yards and return to the car park.

9. There are several excellent viewpoints at Barbury Castle as well as picnic spots to finish off the walk.

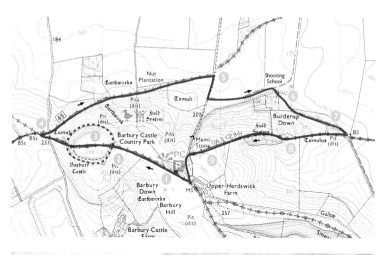

TISBURY

TISBURY IS A HISTORIC VILLAGE IN THE NADDER VALLEY KNOWN FOR ITS LARGE TITHE BARN AND HAS BEEN A SETTLEMENT FOR OVER 2,000 YEARS. AT THE 12TH-CENTURY CHURCH OF ST JOHN THE BAPTIST THE 4,000-YEAR-OLD YEW TREE IS A REMARKABLE SIGHT IN THE VILLAGE.

Most of the older houses in Tisbury are made with local Chilmark stone and the newer high street is characterised by Victorian red brick. This walk takes in the village and heads off to Fonthill Park, which is the setting for one of Wiltshire's more famous tales, before returning to Tisbury.

The imposing Fonthill Estate was purchased by William Beckford in the 18th century. He built the mansion at Fonthill and died in 1770 leaving the estate to his ten-year-old son. The younger William Beckford embraced a life of romanticism, travelling all over Europe and writing books. His love of Gothic romanticism extended to the building of an elaborate dream palace at Fonthill employing over 500 builders. This included a 300-foot (90m) central tower. Beckford lived in the unfinished palace for 15 years before selling the property to John

Farquar, who was a gunpowder millionaire. Eventually the tower collapsed and brought much of the house into disrepair. Today the remains are part of a private house. Fonthill Lake makes a pleasant walk and was the movie setting for some of the river scenes in Chocolat, the film from Joanna Harris's novel.

THE WALK

1. The walk starts in the main car park in Tisbury. Walk back up the road to the High Street and turn right.

2. Continue uphill past shops and the Methodist chapel. On the left-hand side there is a traditional high pavement with steps. Turn left up Weaveland Road and continue walking along the path. This passes Tisbury Swimming Pool. At Tisbury Sports Centre take the footpath to the right between the sports centre and houses.

3. Continue walking along this path towards a farmhouse. Pass the farmhouse and continue straight ahead. Cross into another path that goes across farmland. On the

THE BASICS

Distance: 4 miles / 7km

Gradient: Mainly flat and undulating

Severity: Easy

Approx time: 3 hrs

Stiles: Two

Maps: OS Explorer 143 (Warminster & Trowbridge) and 130 (Salisbury & Stonehenge)

Path description: Mainly footpaths, road, field path

Start point: The Avenue Car Park, Nadder Close, Tisbury (GR ST 945294)

Parking: The Avenue Car Park, Nadder Close, Tisbury (SP3 6JJ)

Dog friendly: Suitable for dogs but keep on a lead near farmland. There is blue green algae at times in Fonthill Lake, making it unsuitable for dogs

Public toilets: At the Avenue Car park in Tisbury

Nearest food: There are several cafes and pubs in Tisbury. The Beckford Arms is on the route and is an option for a break or a visit afterwards right-hand side is a hump-like structure. This is a reservoir and at this point you should turn right up the footpath.

4. Walk up this path and at a junction take the track to the left. Walk ahead to a gate.

5. Continue through the gate on a grassy trail. Go through two kissing gates.

6. Walk along the trail behind houses and at a junction with the road turn right.

7. Walk downhill towards a crossroads. Ahead is a lodge which is part of the Fonthill Estate. On the left is the Beckford Arms.

8. Continue straight across the road and downhill towards Fonthill Lake. On the right-hand side of the road beside a small lay-by is a gap in the hedge. Take this path down through woods towards the lake.

9. Follow the path through the trees with the lake on the left towards a gate. Go through the gate and continue along the marked path.

10. Continue along the path to another gate. This leads out onto a gravel and concreted path and around to the weir. Hydropower has been in existence at Fonthill since 1820 and the pumping station is still in use.

11. Take the path that curves around to the right. Go past the trail on the left that leads uphill and backwards. Veer to the left and go up the footpath ahead of you.

12. At the top go through the field via the path. This path leads around to the right and along the edge of the field. Ahead there is a tree leaning to the right. Just after this marker there is a stile leading into the next field.

13. Climb over the stile and take the path leading downhill through the field. Ahead are lovely views of Tisbury.

14. Cross another stile and continue downhill. At the bottom of the hill turn left along the banks of a stream. Follow this path to a tarmacked lane. At the junction with the road turn left and walk along Duck Street. On the right a road leads to The Avenue.

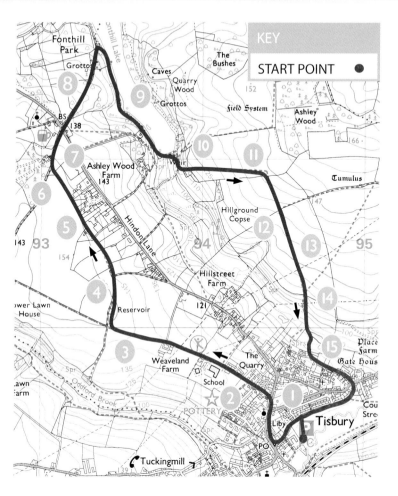

KEY

START POINT ●

15. Cross over into The Avenue and follow this road around. This leads to the car park where the walk began. Once you have completed the walk, Place Farm, where the longest tithe barn in England is located, is a short drive from the centre of Tisbury. Other attractions are the 4,000-year-old yew tree in the churchyard at St John the Baptist Church and the pubs, shops and cafes in Tisbury.

HEYTESBURY

TODAY HEYTESBURY IS A QUIET VILLAGE ON THE
OUTSKIRTS OF WARMINSTER BUT AT ONE TIME IT WAS
LARGE ENOUGH TO SEND TWO MEMBERS OF PARLIAMENT
TO LONDON. THE HISTORIC HOSPITAL OF ST JOHN IS AN
ALMS-HOUSE DATING BACK TO 1449. DURING WORLD
WAR ONE IT WAS A MILITARY HOSPITAL AND TODAY
PROVIDES RESIDENTIAL ACCOMMODATION.

Heytesbury is known for its famous resident, the war poet Siegfried Sassoon who lived for many years at Heytesbury House. The surrounding countryside inspired many of his poems, as of course did the trench warfare in France. This walk takes in the scenic village of Heytesbury and proceeds across Cotley Hill to Scratchbury Camp before descending into Norton Bavant and back to Heytesbury.

One of Siegfried Sassoon's most famous poems is 'On Scratchbury Camp,' about a place where he rode his horse. Walking across this hill the scenery is magnificent and easy to see how it inspired Sassoon. Scratchbury Camp itself is an Iron Age hill fort, and yet another of these magnificent reminders of the ancient defences of the North Wessex Downs.

At the end of the walk the nearby village of Sutton Veny is a short drive away, which has the second largest number of ANZAC war graves in England and is a poignant reminder of the Great War. Many Australians were stationed near here during World War I and several never returned to their homeland.

THE BASICS

Distance: 5 miles / 8km

Gradient: Some inclines but mainly undulating

Severity: Easy

Approx time: 3 hrs

Stiles: Two and two kissing gates

Maps: OS Explorer 143 (Warminster & Trowbridge)

Path description: Mainly footpath and road

Start point: High Street, Heytesbury (GR ST 925426)

Parking: High Street, Heytesbury (BA12 0ED)

Dog friendly: Suitable for dogs but keep on a lead near farmland and around the A36

Public toilets: None on the route but there are toilets for customers of the two pubs

Nearest food: There are two pubs in Heytesbury: the Angel Inn and the Red Lion. A village shop sells snacks

HEYTESBURY WALK

1. Park along the High Street in Heytesbury, taking care not to obstruct entrances. Walk along the street where there is a traditional blind house, used to accommodate drunk and disorderly people in the 18th century. Further along this road is the Hospital of St John Almshouse.

2. At the junction with the road turn left and continue to the main road. The A36 traverses the village. Cross the road carefully as speeds can be deceptive. Go straight ahead up the narrow road.

3. On the right-hand side is the entrance to Heytesbury House, Siegfried Sassoon's old home. This is a private residence. Further up the hill on the left-hand side is a footpath sign marked Imber Range Perimeter Path. Take this path.

4. Continue up this track to a large tree and keep to the right of it. Continue along the path with views on either side.

5. Head along the path towards a wooded area. Go through Cotley Hill Woods.

6. On emerging from the woods, walk ahead on the marked path. This leads to a small tumulus where a cairn has been erected. Continue past the cairn and walk along the path until reaching a gate.

7. Walk through the gate. The views across the hill are superb. Walk across this path and go through another gate.

8. Continue a short distance and on the left take a marked path through a field towards Scratchbury Hill. Walk across to the gate that is the entrance to Scratchbury Camp. The fort is accessible, but do not attempt to descend from the hill at the side opposite to the entrance, especially in wet weather, as the descent is treacherous in parts. Instead, after visiting the fort, return to this gate. Inside the gate, and facing the fort, turn right and follow the ditch.

9. At a fence turn left and go through the gate continuing on the ditch and around the hill fort perimeter. This leads to a footpath on the right.

10. Pick up this footpath and walk over to the right and downhill to a gate. Go through the gate and then walk on the footpath downhill to a lane. Turn left.

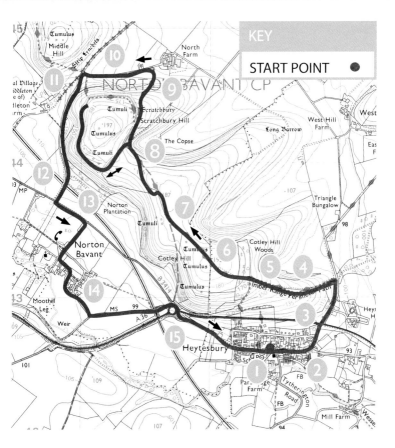

KEY

START POINT ●

11. Walk along this lane past the deserted Middleton Village site, and some houses. Cross the railway bridge and turn left onto a road.

12. Walk up the road using the pavement. At the turning for Norton Bavant turn right. Walk down this road, which has views of Scratchbury Camp. Walk down the road and turn left by the post box into the village.

13. At the end of the path walk onto the road and turn left to the roundabout. This is really busy and should not be crossed by turning right. Instead, cross the roundabout in a clockwise manner until reaching the Heytesbury turnoff. This route has crossing places and there is a lane off the main road for pedestrians at Heytesbury.

14. Walk straight ahead and back into the village.

MARLBOROUGH

The town of Marlborough is located in north-east Wiltshire and is famed for having the widest high street in England. There are markets twice a week here and the 17th-century Merchant's House is a restored silk trader's home.

The town is also famed for Marlborough College, a public school with famous old pupils including the Duchess of Cambridge, Bruce Chatwin and Sir John Betjeman.

The walk takes in the town centre, the hills surrounding Marlborough, and the famous White Horse. Marlborough has one of eight white horses still visible in Wiltshire. This one was cut in 1804 by a group of boys from Mr Greasley's School, which was on the High Street. Each year it was scoured or cleaned, and this became a tradition at the school. When Mr Greasley died in 1830 the horse fell into disrepair but has been restored and is now best seen on the footpath below the village of Preshute. Back in Marlborough there is a wide range of places to eat and drink following the walk.

THE BASICS

Distance: 2 miles / 3.5km

Gradient: Some inclines on the path to the road but mainly flat

Severity: Easy

Approx time: 1 hr

Stiles: Three kissing gates

Maps: OS Explorer 157 (Marlborough & Savernake Forest)

Path description: Footpaths and road

Start point: St Peters Church, High Street (GR SU 187691)

Parking: Hillier's Yard Car Park behind Waitrose (SN8 1BE)

Dog friendly: Suitable for dogs but keep on a lead near the sheep grazing and the busy road

Public toilets: On George Lane, Marlborough

Nearest food: Several places to eat in Marlborough, including the Castle and Ball, Polly's Tea Rooms and St Peter's Church

MARLBOROUGH WALK

1. The walk starts at St Peter's Church on the High Street. This is a disused church and is now a thriving café and art gallery. At the road junction turn left but keep on the left-hand side of the street as this has a pavement on the busy road.

2. Cross the River Kennet via the bridge. At the roundabout a path leads to the right. Take the path that runs alongside some houses.

3. Follow this track until you come to a kissing gate on the left. Go through the gate and follow the path up to a second gate. This is steep and emerges on the hill, which is a very busy road.

4. Turn right and walk up the road for about 100 yards to the footpath on the right. Keep on the verge as much as possible due to the oncoming traffic.

5. At the start of this footpath there are some ancient earthworks. There are also some splendid views across the town of Marlborough. Walk along this path with views to the right.

6. Before the wooded area take the footpath downhill marked White Horse Trail towards a sports centre.

7. Turn right down a path besides some tennis courts and sports tracks which are part of Marlborough College. On the right is the Marlborough White Horse. It is thin looking and at one time this was a more solid feature but has become more streamlined over the years.

8. Continue on this path to the end. Turn left and head back into Marlborough.

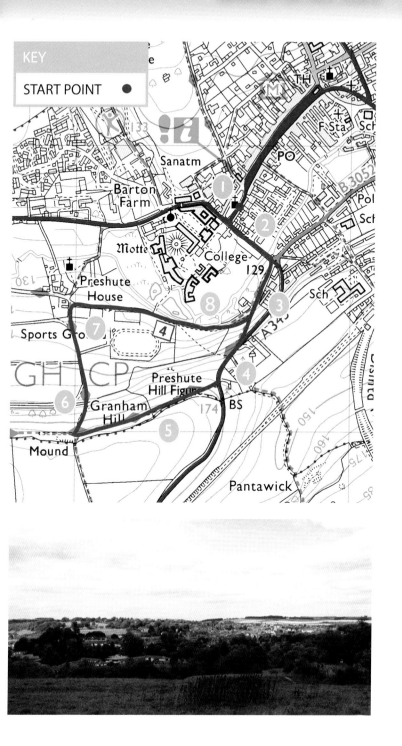

KEY

START POINT ●

DURRINGTON

One of the most intriguing things about Stonehenge and Durrington is that new theories and discoveries are being made all the time about the area. Around 4,500 years ago this entire area was a huge settlement and place of worship and its significance is still a matter of historical debate.

The walk leads from Durrington past Woodhenge and through ancient paths to the main Avenue itself at Stonehenge. Durrington Walls was the site of a large settlement or village in Neolithic times and was characterised by henges or earth banks which enclosed timber circles. It is thought that up to 300 homes were here at the time. Some theories suggest that Durrington represented the land of the living and that outside the boundary was the place of the dead. Durrington means the land of the doers, signifying life and it is known that livestock were kept here in Neolithic times.

Woodhenge is a representation of the timber circles that once stood here and which were aligned to the sun movements. This site may have been a transition point between life and death. The Kings Barrow is characterised by burial mounds beneath beech trees and leads the way to the Avenue as the main approach to Stonehenge. This is thought to have been the main ceremonial approach to Stonehenge, characterised by earth banks. Stonehenge itself is one of the most famous stone circles in the world and is believed to be around 5,000 years old.

THE BASICS

Distance: 4 miles / 6km

Gradient: Mainly flat

Severity: Easy

Approx time: 2 hrs

Stiles: None

Maps: OS Explorer 130 (Salisbury & Stonehenge)

Path description: Some mud tracks, fields and paths

Start point: Woodhenge, Amesbury (GR SU 151433)

Parking: Car park or roadside at Woodhenge (SP4 7AR)

Dog friendly: Suitable for dogs but keep on a lead near livestock

Public toilets: None

Nearest food: Nearest pub is Stonehenge Inn in Durrington

DURRINGTON WALK

1. Begin the walk at the Woodhenge Car Park in Durrington. Ahead is the earthwork bank and the historic site of Durrington Walls.

2. Cross the path beside the car park to Woodhenge and spend a few moments at the timber site which depicts how the structure may have looked in Neolithic times. At the gate turn left and continue along the track. In the next field to the left is the Cuckoo Stone. This is a large sarsen stone, believed to have occurred naturally in its location before being upended.

3. Walk into the housing estate and on the left is a footpath sign. Take this path.

4. Continue down the track and turn to the right where the main Long Barrow path joins this trail. Walk along this historic trail, which is lined with wild fruit trees and bushes. The Cursus in this area was a rectangular earth bank that predates Stonehenge. Its function in religious rites remains unknown.

5. The path emerges at some houses and to the left is a tree-lined avenue. This is the Kings Barrow where there are a number of burial mounds beneath the beech trees. Walk along this path to a gate on the right-hand size.

6. Continue walking along this path with views of Stonehenge until arriving at a gate on the right. This marks the entrance to the Avenue.

7. Walk up the Avenue to see Stonehenge's stone circle before retracing your steps to the gate. Please note, this is not an entry point to the main visitor centre but just a viewpoint.

8. Walk back through the Kings Barrow to the gate. Turn right. At the junction in the lane turn left.

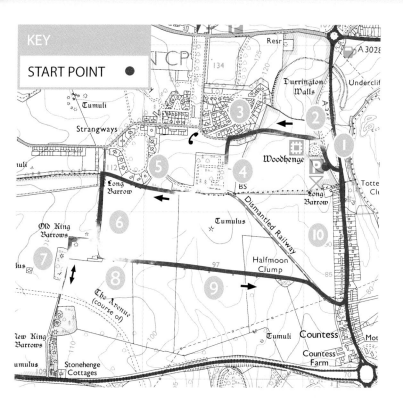

9. Continue along this track. To the right are the Nile Clumps reputed to have been planted by Charles Douglas - 6th Marquess of Queensberry, a friend of Lady Hamilton. Each clump of trees is said to represent the position of a ship as given on a map by Robert Dodd.

10. Walk to the end of the lane. At the junction with the road turn left and continue to the Woodhenge Car Park on the left-hand side. As an option for learning more about the area after the walk, the Stonehenge Visitor Centre is a short drive from Durrington and has an admission charge.

BRADFORD-ON-AVON

BRADFORD-ON-AVON IS A UNIQUE TOWN FULL OF ARCHITECTURAL TREASURES FROM MEDIEVAL TITHE BARNS TO 17TH-CENTURY CLOTHIERS' HOMES AND WEAVERS' COTTAGES. IT IS BISECTED BY THE RIVER AVON WITH A WEIR RUNNING THROUGH THE TOWN AT GREENLAND MILL AND WITH BUILDINGS STACKED INTO THE HILLSIDES.

The focus of this market town is the ancient packhorse bridge which still has two original 13th-century arches and was once a crossing without parapets – so people frequently fell off. Unusually there is a blind house built into the bridge structure itself. This walk takes in the historic centre and continues out along the famous Kennet and Avon Canal before returning into the town.

The canal is mainly full of touring barges today but at one time this was a busy industrial thoroughfare. The High Wharf was once a busy trading depot between Bath and London and was a storage base for goods that ended up being shipped all over the world. Walk further down the towpath and there are homes on the water complete with rooftop vegetable gardens and decorative signage. At Bradford-on-Avon the canal follows the south side of the Avon Valley with steep sides where the river has cut into limestone. Clay found on the rock beds here is known as Bradford clay, and William Smith was prominent in identifying many fossil species and geological features of this area.

THE BASICS

Distance: 4 miles / 7km

Gradient: Some inclines but mainly flat. A steep descent down St Margaret's Steps

Severity: Easy

Approx time: 3 hrs

Stiles: None

Maps: OS Explorer 156 (Chippenham & Bradford-on-Avon)

Path description: Canal towpath, fields and paths

Start point: Station car park, Frome Road (GR ST 825607)

Parking: Station car park, (BA15 1DQ) & St Margaret's Street Car Park (BA15 1DE)

Dog friendly: Suitable for dogs but keep on a lead near farmland

Public toilets: St Margaret's Street Car Park. The Lock Inn Café allows its toilet to be used by the public during opening hours

Nearest food: The Lock Inn Café is on Frome Road. There are several other pubs, restaurants and tea rooms in town

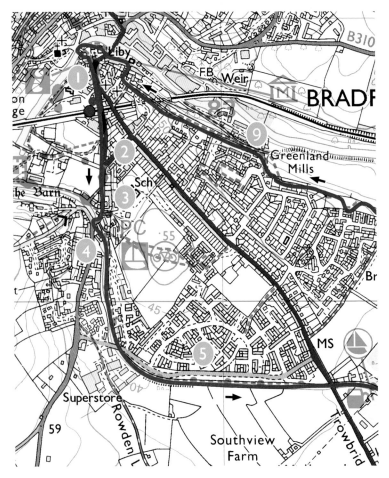

1. This walk commences in the Bradford-on-Avon railway station car park. Walk out of the car park and turn right. Continue down Frome Road past shops to a junction marked 'Tithe Barn' on the right.

2. Walk down this lane to the 14th-century Tithe Barn owned by English Heritage. The magnificent beamed ceilings have been dated back to the 14th century. There are also craft shops and galleries in this area. Walk back up the lane and turn right. Continue down the road to the bridge and a marked footpath sign on the left.

3. Walk down to the canal towpath. On the left is an information centre about the canal. Walk straight ahead down this path passing narrow boats, day boats and life on the canal.

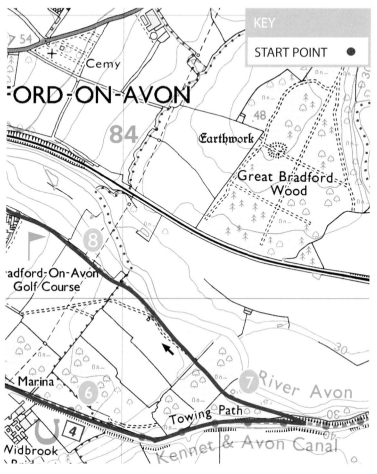

KEY

START POINT •

4. Pass two bridges and a marina on the right. Further down is a marked footpath on the left-hand side. This leads down a track to the River Avon.

5. Follow the path down to the river and around to the left along a grassy track to a field. This opens into a larger area but keep on the track until coming to a field gate.

6. Go through the gate into the field and walk across it staying on the marked footpath.

Go through a second field and into a third, walking towards a housing estate.

7. Take the narrow passageway out of the field and ahead. This leads to a road. Follow this road around to the left and to a sign named Mythern Meadow. Straight ahead of you is a house in the right-hand corner of the housing estate. To the right of this house is a footpath. Take this path which leads to some garages.

8. Walk to the left of the garages and then stay on the road walking ahead. Opposite the house numbered 15 there is a track leading down to a wide footpath. Walk down the track and turn left. Continue walking on this path through a wooded area and behind houses.

9. On reaching the Scout Hut there are some lovely views of Bradford-on-Avon. To the right are St Margaret's Steps, which lead down to the town centre. There are lots of cafes and places to see in Bradford on Avon, but otherwise continue walking ahead and to the right which takes you back to the station car park.

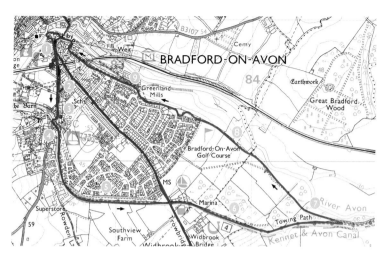

MALMESBURY

When John Betjeman visited Malmesbury he wrote, 'You wouldn't know, driving through Malmesbury, what a sacred and peculiar place it is. You wouldn't know what gives it an atmosphere you can almost touch and see.'

Malmesbury is a Saxon hilltop town standing between two branches of the River Avon and is one of the oldest boroughs in England. In AD 880 King Alfred granted a royal charter to the town. It has a medieval street plan and the remains of a Benedictine abbey founded by St Aldhelm in the 7th century. Amongst its features are the tomb of King Athelstan, who made Malmesbury his capital, and the Norman porch. There are many historic houses here and hilly streets to explore with riverside walks and the iconic Market Cross.

Malmesbury grew wealthy on the wool trade and was also known for producing fine silk in the mills. The walk starts in the town centre and weaves out towards the fields, returning via Twatley to the town. En route it crosses several of the town's historic bridges which are a feature of Malmesbury. The Abbey Gardens are a popular attraction in Malmesbury and can be visited after the walk.

THE BASICS

Distance: 4 miles / 7km

Gradient: Some inclines but mainly undulating. A steep ascent into town at the end

Severity: See notes on the two stiles with Cotswold stones where the road is a possible alternative

Approx time: 3 hrs

Stiles: Four

Maps: OS Explorer 168 (Stroud, Tetbury & Malmesbury)

Path description: Some mud tracks, fields and paths

Start point: West Gate Bridge, Malmesbury (GR ST 932875)

Parking: Station Road, Malmesbury (SN16 9JT)

Dog friendly: Suitable for dogs but keep on a lead near farmland and roads

Public toilets: In the Town Hall, Malmesbury

Nearest food: Several pubs and cafes in Malmesbury

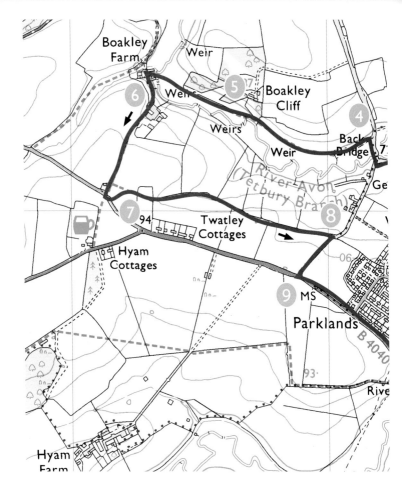

1. The walk starts at a plaque, in the pavement in front of the Old Bell Hotel, which marks the site of the town's West Gate. Walk down the hill towards a stone cross. At this junction take the road to the right.

2. Walk downhill past several stone cottages. At the bottom of the hill a metal bridge crosses the Avon. This is Stainsbridge which was widened during the 1970s and replaced the original 13th century crossing. Do not cross the bridge to continue the walk but carry on around the road.

3. Walk past houses and at Park Road turn right. At the end of this road continue ahead up a path beside the river. Eventually this leads to Back Bridge. Cross this bridge.

KEY

START POINT ●

4. To the left, take the footpath which crosses a field. There is a shed here with some interesting street art.

5. Cross the field to a stile. This leads into a field and immediately to the left is a gate. Go through the gate and walk ahead to the farmyard.

6. Walk through the farmyard and around to the left to a track. Walk along this and at some farm sheds take the track to the right.

7. Walk down this track to the road. An alternative to the footpath route described below is to continue walking back into Malmesbury on this road but taking care with busy traffic. On the road, immediately to the left is a footpath sign. Go over the stile and walk across the field towards the right to another stile. Go across this stile.

8. Walk across the field to another stile, taking care with the wood crossing as it goes over a ditch and has a large Cotswold style stone on the other side.

9. Go through this field to the next stile which also crosses a ditch with a similar stone feature so care needs to be taken. Cross two more fields keeping to the left side.

10. At a junction with a lane turn right. Walk to the end and to the main road.

11. Turn left and walk straight ahead. Continue past the school. On the right-hand side a narrow road goes downhill. Take this road to the bridge and cross it. On the left is a footpath sign. Walk across the field with Malmesbury ahead of you. Cross the clapper bridge at Daniel's Well and continue following the path back into town. This leads up to the right and then up some steep steps to the town centre.

12. Back in town there are lots of cafes to enjoy or visit the Abbey and gardens.

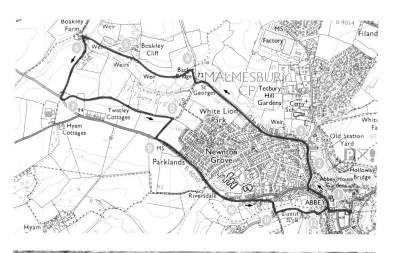

ROUNDWAY HILL

On 16 July 1643 the most decisive battle of the English Civil War took place above Devizes on Roundway Down. The Royalist victory opened up the opportunity to sweep out of the South West towards London and change the course of the war.

After a failed battle at Lansdowne the Royalist troops were holed up in the town of Devizes, hotly pursued by Cromwell's army. A weakened Lord Ralph Hopton sent Prince Maurice to Oxford in search of reinforcements for the battle to come. The Parliamentarian leader Lord Waller continued besieging Devizes, unaware that more troops were on the way. Eventually, with news that more Royalists were en route, Waller took his army, known as the 'Lobsters', up onto Roundway Hill where they clashed with Lord Wilmot's brigade. The Royalists charged twice and forced the Parliamentarians over towards Oliver's Castle.

The fleeing Parliamentarian army were unaware of the treacherous steep sides of Oliver's Castle as they were forced to the edge. Over 300 men and horses broke their necks as they charged down the steep 300-foot drop and were killed. There were now no more Parliamentarian forces left in the South West, giving the Royalists the upper hand. This walk takes in the battle sites of Roundway Down and sweeping views of the countryside surrounding it.

NOTE: The car park is best approached from Roundway as the other approaches are not suited to some cars. The Rowdey Cow Café and Ice Cream Parlour, café overlooks Roundway Hill and is open from 10:00 to 17:00 daily.

THE BASICS

Distance: 4 miles / 7km

Gradient: Mainly flat. A steep ascent back to the car park at the end.

Severity: Easy

Approx time: 2–3 hrs

Stiles: Two kissing gates

Maps: OS Explorer 157 (Marlborough & Savernake Forest)

Path description: Some mud tracks, fields and paths

Start point: White Horse car Park, Roundway Hill (GR SU 014637)

Parking: White Horse car Park, Roundway Hill. Nearest postcode: SN10 2HZ, which is Roundway Farm (south of the car park)

Dog friendly: Suitable for dogs but keep on a lead near farmland

Public toilets: None

Nearest food: Rowdey Cow Café and Ice Cream Parlour, Lower Farm, Devizes Road, Rowde, Devizes, SN10 2LX

ROUNDWAY HILL WALK

1. This walk starts in the White Horse car park on Roundway Hill. There is a viewpoint here beside the Devizes White Horse.

2. Walk up the byway away from the car park entrance. Ancient tumuli can be seen in the fields to the right of this track. Further along are marker points of the Battle of Roundway Down where the troops gathered and charged in 1643.

3. At the crossroads of the byways turn left. Continue up this track. Further up this byway is a viewing point on the left which gives a view of the historic battle charge area.

4. Continue up the road past a junction with a road and go straight ahead.

5. Take the footpath ahead which is marked by dragon's teeth. Walk up this lane and take the footpath to the left. Views of Oliver's Castle emerge and this is one of the points where the retreating army would have been escaping in 1643.

6. Pass the first gate in the fence and go to the second gate on the right where there is a footpath sign. Walk across the path to Oliver's Castle where there are beautiful views.

7. Walk across the castle on the footpath and at the far end is the Bloody Ditch, a steep drop where over 300 soldiers and horses charged to their deaths.

8. Follow the path to the left and continue along the ditch, keeping to the trail. Take the footpath to a clearing and a small parking area.

9. Take the Mid Wilts Way to the right and continue up this track to a junction with a road.

10. Walk along this road which has views from the right-hand side. At a fork in the road turn sharp left.

11. Walk back up the steep hill to the White Horse Car Park and the end of the walk. More about the Battle of Roundway Down can be found in Devizes Museum.

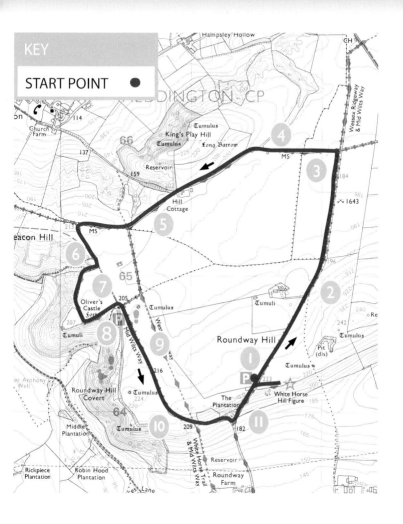

ABOUT THE AUTHOR

Rachael Rowe is a writer specialising in travel and health and lives in Dorset. Her publications include online and print travel articles. Walking is a particular interest and the area in North Dorset where she lives is full of places to roam. She also works in the NHS, specialising in cardiovascular disease, and is fully aware of the benefits of walking for health.

Rachael is originally from Cornwall and has travelled to over 50 countries, many with classic walking trails, and has also lived in Switzerland.

The West Country is a particular favourite place to walk on weekends and she has enjoyed creating this book so that others can get out and about and discover what Wiltshire has to offer.

Her portfolio can be seen at www.rachaelrowe.com